I. INTRODUCTION

On July 8, 2011, the Office of the Inspector General (OIG) received information from an attorney representing John Dodson, a Special Agent with the Bureau of Alcohol, Tobacco, Firearms and Explosives (ATF), concerning the alleged unauthorized disclosure of sensitive ATF information. According to Dodson's attorney, Dodson had received an e-mail from a Fox News producer asking for comment about excerpts from an internal ATF investigative memorandum that Dodson had drafted and which described a proposed undercover operation for an ATF firearms investigation (the Dodson memorandum or memorandum).

Dodson's attorney alleged that officials within the Department of Justice (Department or DOJ) had disclosed the memorandum to retaliate against Dodson for his criticism of the conduct of the firearms trafficking investigation referred to as Operation Fast and Furious. On June 15, 2011, shortly before the alleged unauthorized disclosure, Dodson and other ATF agents had expressed their concerns about Operation Fast and Furious during testimony before the U.S. House of Representatives Committee on Oversight and Government Reform.[1]

The OIG initiated an investigation of the alleged unauthorized disclosure of the Dodson memorandum shortly after receiving this complaint. We determined early in the investigation that the memorandum was among documents the Department had produced to or made available for review by the U.S. Senate Committee on the Judiciary and the U.S. House of Representatives Committee on Oversight and Government Reform in connection with their investigation of Operation Fast and Furious. We requested the Department components that had a role in the document production to Congress to identify all personnel whose official responsibilities required or permitted their access to these documents. In response to this request, we received the names of 152 employees in 8 Department components, including Dennis Burke, who was then the United States Attorney for the District of Arizona.

On August 16, 2011, Burke contacted an OIG investigative counsel by telephone and said that he had released the Dodson memorandum to

---

[1] The OIG's November 2012 report, *A Review of ATF's Operation Fast and Furious and Related Matters*, can be found at http://www.justice.gov/oig/reports/2012/s1209.pdf.

a reporter.[2] Burke also stated that the reporter already seemed to be familiar with the contents of the Dodson memorandum before Burke provided it to him. Burke further told the OIG investigative counsel that he was at the airport preparing to board a flight and would be on vacation the following week, but that he would meet with the OIG for an interview when he returned.[3] However, Burke resigned as U.S. Attorney on August 29, 2011, and declined the OIG's subsequent requests for an interview.[4]

In light of Burke's claim that the reporter seemed to be familiar with the contents of the Dodson memorandum before Burke provided it to him, the OIG continued its investigation. We requested signed declarations from 150 of the 152 employees who had been identified by the Department as having had access to the documents produced or made available to Congress.[5] In the declarations, employees answered under oath several questions about their knowledge of or participation in the unauthorized disclosure of the Dodson memorandum to the media. All 150 employees executed and returned the declaration, and based on their responses, we interviewed five officials who stated in their declarations that they had some direct knowledge about the disclosure. We also reviewed the official e-mail accounts of relevant Department officials and issued an administrative subpoena to a communications service provider to identify the subscriber of a personal e-mail address.

In Section II of this report, we provide background information about the Dodson memorandum and the Department policies that govern the disclosure of information to the media by Department officials, including U.S. Attorneys. Section III describes our factual findings concerning the disclosure of the Dodson memorandum. We also include in this section a description of relevant information the Department

---

[2] The U.S. Attorney's Office for the District of Arizona was originally responsible for prosecuting subjects identified in Operation Fast and Furious. That responsibility was transferred to the U.S. Attorney's Office for the Southern District of California in September 2011.

[3] The OIG investigative counsel memorialized Burke's admission in an e-mail to OIG management immediately after the telephone call.

[4] On December 13, 2011, Burke was interviewed by congressional investigators about several matters pertaining to Operation Fast and Furious, including his disclosure of the Dodson memorandum to a reporter. At the OIG's request, the staff of the House Committee on Oversight and Government Reform provided a copy of Burke's transcribed interview and we cite to testimony Burke provided to congressional investigators in this report.

[5] The two individuals who did not execute declarations were Burke and a Department employee who died.

learned during its review of another disclosure to the media in the summer of 2011 of confidential Department information relating to Operation Fast and Furious. Section IV sets forth our analysis and conclusions.

II.   BACKGROUND

A.   The Dodson Memorandum

In 2009, Special Agent Dodson was transferred to ATF's Phoenix Division where he was assigned to the group responsible for conducting the Operation Fast and Furious investigation. In addition to his involvement with that case, Dodson conducted an investigation involving an individual suspected of trafficking firearms. In May 2010, Dodson drafted and e-mailed a memorandum to his supervisor that proposed an operation in which Dodson would act in an undercover capacity as a straw purchaser and deliver firearms to the suspected firearms trafficker but take no enforcement action upon delivery.[6]

The proposal was approved by Assistant Special Agent in Charge James Needles, and on June 1, 2010, Dodson purchased six firearms from two licensed gun retailers and then sold the guns to the suspect. After the sale was completed, other ATF agents followed the suspect to a gated storage facility and then terminated their surveillance. In August 2010, the suspect told Dodson, who was still acting in his undercover capacity, that he was no longer in the business of obtaining firearms from straw purchasers and reselling them for profit. In October 2010, Dodson met with the suspect and identified himself as an ATF agent and conducted an interview. The suspect told Dodson he no longer possessed the six firearms. The case was subsequently closed and the suspect was not arrested.

---

[6] As described in our report, *A Review of ATF's Operation Fast and Furious and Related Matters* (November 2012), Dodson told us he was frustrated with Operation Fast and Furious because he did not understand how conducting surveillances of what appeared to be unlawful firearms purchases and transfers without taking any enforcement action – such as seizing the firearms – was a viable or responsible approach to developing the case. Dodson told us he and other agents had joked that ATF should sell firearms directly to the subject of Dodson's investigation, and that he then decided to propose the undercover operation described in the May 2010 memorandum. According to Dodson, he and the other agents thought that the proposal would be rejected and that when the managers saw such a plan in "black and white" they would be shocked into realizing what they were doing in Operation Fast and Furious. Dodson said that after his plan was approved he reluctantly went forward with it and that he still regretted delivering the firearms to the subject and letting them "walk."

B.   Applicable Department Regulations

As described later in this report, Burke admitted to disclosing the Dodson memorandum to a member of the media and we did not identify any other individuals who disclosed the document, or the information contained in the document, to a member of the media. We therefore describe below those Department regulations that were applicable to Burke's conduct.

The disclosure of the Dodson memorandum was subject to Department guidelines and policies that govern interactions with and the release of investigative information to members of the media. The U.S. Attorney's Manual (USAM) Section 1-7.210, *General Responsibility,* provides:

> Final responsibility for all matters involving the news media and the Department of Justice is vested in the Director of the Office of Public Affairs (OPA). The Attorney General is to be kept fully informed of appropriate matters at all times. Responsibility for all matters involving the local media is vested in the United States Attorney.

USAM Section 1-7.320 states that in cases of national importance, U.S. Attorneys must consult with OPA about media relations:

> Recognizing that each of the 93 United States Attorneys will exercise independent discretion as to matters affecting their own districts, the United States Attorneys are responsible for coordinating their news media efforts with the Director of OPA in cases that transcend their immediate district or are of national importance.

USAM Section 1-7.330, *Requests from National Media Representatives,* states that communications with national media organizations must be coordinated with OPA:

> In order to promote coordination with the OPA, all components of the Department shall take all reasonable steps to insure compliance with the following . . . OPA should be informed immediately of all requests from national media organizations . . . regarding in-depth stories and matters affecting the Department of Justice, or matters of national significance.

Finally, USAM Section 1-7.401, Guidance for Press Conferences and other Media Contacts, provides:

Prior to conducting a press conference or making comments on a pending investigation regarding another DOJ component, the U.S. Attorney shall coordinate any comments, including any written statements, with the affected component.

III. OIG FACTUAL FINDINGS

A. Congress requests information and documents from Department regarding Operation Fast and Furious

On January 27, 2011, Senator Charles E. Grassley, Ranking Member of the Senate Judiciary Committee, wrote to then-ATF Acting Director Kenneth Melson raising concerns about "an ATF operation called 'Project Gunrunner.'" Among the concerns described in the letter were allegations that ATF had "sanctioned the sale of hundreds of assault weapons to suspected straw purchasers" – individuals who acquire firearms from a federal licensed dealer for the purpose of concealing the identity of the true intended receiver of the firearms. The letter stated that the straw purchasers then transported these weapons throughout the southwest border area and into Mexico, and that two of these weapons were used in a December 14, 2010, firefight that resulted in the death of Customs and Border Protection (CBP) Agent Brian Terry. Although the letter nowhere mentioned Operation Fast and Furious, ATF and Department officials told us that they understood Sen. Grassley's references to Project Gunrunner to mean Operation Fast and Furious.

Over the course of the next several weeks, Sen. Grassley sought information and documents from the Department relating to Operation Fast and Furious. On February 16, Sen. Grassley wrote the Attorney General requesting four specific categories of documents, including all communications between ATF and the Federal Firearms Licensee (FFL) who sold the two firearms found at the scene of Agent Terry's death and all records relating to communications between ATF Headquarters and the Special Agent in Charge of the Phoenix field office. The Department responded by letter dated March 2, stating, "we are not in a position to disclose documents relating to any ongoing investigation, nor can we confirm or deny the existence of records in our ongoing investigative files, based upon the Department's longstanding policy regarding pending matters."[7]

---

[7] The Department's letter also stated that the Attorney General had asked the Acting Inspector General to conduct an investigation into the concerns raised about Operation Fast and Furious.

As the discussion between the Department and Sen. Grassley about access to documents was ongoing, on March 3, 2011, CBS News published an article based on an on-the-record interview of Dodson conducted by reporter Sharyl Attkisson. The article was accompanied by a video that included excerpts from the interview. In that interview, Dodson told Attkisson that ATF was intentionally allowing firearms to go to Mexico, a tactic referred to as "walking" guns. Dodson said he was ordered by his supervisors not to take any action to stop the firearms and that the tactic was approved by Department officials. Dodson also stated that he felt ATF was partly to blame for the escalating violence in Mexico and along the border. The CBS story reported that Sen. Grassley began investigating Operation Fast and Furious after his office spoke to Dodson and several other ATF sources. With respect to access to documents, Sen. Grassley told Attkisson that, "From the standpoint of documents we want – we have not gotten them. I think it is a case of stonewalling."

On March 16, Representative Darrell E. Issa, Chairman of the House Committee on Oversight and Government Reform, wrote to Acting Director Melson to raise concerns about ATF's cooperation with Sen. Grassley's requests for information regarding Project Gunrunner and Operation Fast and Furious, and to request that Melson provide the Committee on Oversight and Government Reform with substantially similar documents and information by March 30, 2011. On March 31, 2011, Representative Issa issued a congressional subpoena to Acting Director Melson for the documents referenced in his March 16 letter.[8] In order to respond to this and other Congressional requests for documents relating to Operation Fast and Furious, the Department established a process for categorizing and producing potentially responsive ATF documents.

According to the Chief of the ATF's Office of Strategic Management, the process involved Department attorneys and ATF agents reviewing documents to determine whether they were responsive to the subpoena, followed by Department officials determining whether a responsive document should be given to Congress, made available for review at the Department (but not produced), or withheld from Congress based on a specific privilege. Those documents identified for production to Congress were further examined to determine whether redactions were necessary.

---

[8] On April 1, 2011, the Department wrote a letter to Representative Issa stating that it was "surprised and disappointed when shortly after we notified your staff of our intent to work with the Committee, you nevertheless issued a subpoena a few hours later." The letter stated that the Department had informed Committee staff on March 31 that it intended to produce some responsive documents within the next week.

After documents were processed in this manner, they were uploaded for storage into a dedicated shared network drive that was accessible to authorized Department personnel.

On April 5, 2011, Arizona U.S. Attorney's Office Criminal Division Chief Patrick Cunningham, who was assisting in the review of Operation Fast and Furious documents for production to Congress, sent an e-mail to Associate Deputy Attorney General Matthew Axelrod and copied Burke and several other lawyers in the Department's Criminal Division and the U.S. Attorney's Office. Cunningham attached two e-mails from Dodson, including one that Dodson had sent to his supervisor forwarding the memorandum containing the undercover proposal. Cunningham wrote,

> enclosed are the two Dodson e-mails I spoke of last week on our call regarding the Issa letter, now subpoena . . . it seem [sic] to me that these e-mails may be responsive to the subpoena paragraph 8 which asks for documents regarding the 'failure to maintain operational control over weapons purchased by known or suspected straw buyers . . .' What do you think?[9]

One of the recipients of the e-mail commented, "And **that's** his whistleblower?" (emphasis in original) Burke replied,

> Yep. Unbelievable. This guy called Grassley and CBS to unearth what he in fact was proposing to do by himself. When you thought the hypocrisy of this whole matter had hit the limit already . . .

On April 20, 2011, Assistant U.S. Attorney Emory Hurley sent an e-mail to Cunningham with a copy to Burke about one of several attachments to an earlier letter that Sen. Grassley had sent to the Department. In that letter, Sen. Grassley described what he considered "mounting evidence" his office had received that ATF had allowed firearms to "walk," and reiterated his request for information and documents about Operation Fast and Furious. Hurley described one of the attachments to Sen. Grassley's letter as consisting of

---

[9] Paragraph 8 of the congressional subpoena requested,

Documents and communications relating to complaints or objections by ATF agents about: (1) encouraging, sanctioning, or otherwise allowing FFLs to sell firearms to known or suspected straw buyers, (2) failure to maintain surveillance on known or suspected straw buyers, (3) failure to maintain operational control over weapons purchased by known or suspected straw buyers, or (4) letting known or suspected straw buyers with American guns enter Mexico.

redacted reports from [an] ATF case . . . This was an
operation that John Dodson was running. Dodson got
approval from ATF ASAC Needles to allow guns to go to the
suspect. The [U.S. Attorney's Office] did not approve this
investigation. The reports are not part of Fast and Furious.

The attachments in fact were reports of investigation from Dodson's case
that described the conduct of the undercover operation proposed in the
Dodson memorandum.

The Department made a redacted version of the Dodson
memorandum available to Congressional investigators on June 21, 2011,
as part of a larger production of documents. Congressional investigators
were not permitted to make a copy of the memorandum but could only
review it in Department of Justice office space. On June 22, 2011, the
Department provided a version of the Dodson memorandum to the U.S.
Attorney's Office that indicated the redactions that had been made before
making it available for Congressional investigators.

B. Unauthorized disclosure of Avila memorandum and the testimony of ATF special agents before Congress

On June 14, 2011, The New York Times published an article on its
website about a joint report to be released that same day by the House
Committee on Oversight and Government Reform and Senate Judiciary
Committee about Operation Fast and Furious.[10] The article discussed
an internal U.S. Attorney's Office memorandum dated January 28, 2011,
addressed to Burke from Assistant U.S. Attorney Hurley concerning
Operation Fast and Furious suspect Jaime Avila (the Avila
memorandum).[11] The article also included a hyperlink to an image of the
memorandum. We were advised by Department investigators that the
Department had not produced the memorandum or made it available to
Congressional investigators before it appeared on The New York Times
website.

The following day, on June 15, 2011, the House Committee on
Oversight and Government Reform held a hearing entitled, "*Operation*

---

[10] The June 14, 2011, Joint Staff Report is entitled, "The Department of
Justice's Operation Fast and Furious: Accounts of ATF Agents," and is available to the
public at http://oversight.house.gov/wp-content/uploads/2012/02/ATF_Report.pdf.

[11] Two firearms purchased by Avila on January 16, 2010, were recovered at the
scene of the December 14, 2010, shooting death of Customs and Border Protection
Agent Brian Terry.

Fast and Furious: Reckless Decisions, Tragic Outcomes." Dodson and two other ATF agents testified at the hearing.[12]

The agents' testimony was sharply critical of ATF and the U.S. Attorney's Office for the District of Arizona. Dodson's criticism focused on ATF and what he claimed was the investigative technique used in Operation Fast and Furious of monitoring suspected straw purchases of firearms without interdicting to seize the weapons, a practice he and others referred to as "gun walking." Dodson testified,

> Simply put, during this operation referred to as "Fast and Furious," we, the ATF, failed to fulfill one of our most fundamental obligations: to caretake the public trust, in part to keep guns out of the hands of criminals. . . . Prior to my coming to Phoenix, I had never been involved in or even heard of an operation in which law enforcement officers would let guns walk. The very idea of doing so is unthinkable to most law enforcement . . . I cannot begin to think of how the risk of letting guns fall into the hands of known criminals could possibly advance any legitimate law enforcement interest. No one in ATF involved in this, up to Acting Director Melson, has shown any significant leadership in this matter.

A second ATF agent gave testimony that was similarly critical of ATF and the U.S. Attorney's Office. The agent testified,

> What we have here is actually a colossal failure in leadership, from within ATF, within the chain-of-command involved in this case, within the U.S. Attorney's Office, and within DOJ, as to the individuals who are aware of this strategy. To walk a single gun is, in my opinion, an idiotic move. . . . This was a catastrophic disaster.

With regard to the U.S. Attorney's Office, the second agent accused the attorneys responsible for federal firearms prosecutions of giving a pass to dozens of firearms traffickers by declining to prosecute their cases despite the existence of probable cause. The agent cited "either laziness or arrogance" as the underlying cause of the U.S. Attorney's Office refusals to prosecute ATF firearms cases, and said that as a

---

[12] The complete transcript of the hearing is available to the public at http://oversight.house.gov/hearing/operation-fast-and-furious-reckless-decisions-tragic-outcomes/.

consequence, ATF often turned to state prosecutors to pursue cases against firearms traffickers. According to the agent,

> Due to the recalcitrance of the U.S. Attorney's Office, cases such as these were presented for prosecution to the Arizona Attorney General's Office, where State laws carried significantly lesser penalties than they did under the Federal statutes.

On June 16, 2011, the day after the Congressional hearing, Deputy Attorney General James Cole contacted Burke by telephone to discuss the apparent unauthorized disclosure of the Avila memorandum that had appeared on The New York Times website on June 14. As described above, The New York Times article included a hyperlink to an image of the actual Avila memorandum. That image included a banner indicating the document had been transmitted by facsimile from the U.S. Attorney's Office in Arizona: "Jun-14-2011 02:21 PM S Attys Office – Arizona 602-514-7683." The telephone number displayed in the banner is registered to the Arizona U.S. Attorney's Office.[13]

According to Department investigators, Cole informed Burke in their June 16th conversation that the matter was being referred to the Office of Professional Responsibility (OPR). Cole asked Burke if he knew how the memorandum was obtained by The New York Times, and Burke told him that only five or six people had access to the document but that he, Burke, did not even know whether his office had a facsimile machine.

Department investigators contacted Burke by telephone on June 24, 2011, to gather preliminary information regarding the leak. During that call, Burke stated that he might be able to obviate the need for an OPR investigation because as head of the U.S. Attorney's Office he was ultimately responsible for the actions of his staff. Burke was asked whether he had authorized the release of the memorandum to The New York Times. According to Department investigators, Burke's answer was not clear or unambiguous.

Additionally, Department investigators told us that three days later, on June 27, 2011, Cole made a second telephone call to Burke about the disclosure of the Avila memorandum. Cole said that Burke confirmed he had accepted responsibility for the leak of the Avila

---

[13] Shortly after The New York Times published the story with the link to the Avila memorandum, the document originally linked to the story had been changed to redact the U.S. Attorney's Office's fax machine information stamped on the top of the pages of the memorandum.

memorandum and acknowledged he had not been candid with Cole during their first conversation. Cole also reported that Burke said the Avila memorandum was provided to The New York Times by the press person in the U.S. Attorney's Office, but that Burke could not say that it was his (Burke's) idea. Cole also said he could not get a clear answer from Burke about whether he had authorized the release of the Avila memorandum or was simply accepting responsibility for it because he was the head of the office. Cole said that he believed Burke was being evasive during this portion of the conversation. Burke subsequently declined to answer further questions from the Department about this incident.

Cole told the OIG that he placed the second telephone call to Burke after he learned that, contrary to what Burke indicated during the first telephone call, Burke was involved with the disclosure of the Avila memorandum. Cole said he called Burke "to chastise him for (a) lying to me and (b) leaking . . ." Cole also told us that he put Burke on notice that such disclosures should not occur.[14]

C. Burke provides Dodson memorandum to Fox News

Burke told Congressional investigators that in "very late June" – around June 29 – he was contacted by Fox News reporter Mike Levine, whom Burke said he had known for approximately 1½ years.[15] According to records reviewed by the OIG, Burke and Levine occasionally exchanged e-mails and sometimes met when Burke traveled to Washington, D.C., where Levine was assigned to cover the Department. Burke told congressional investigators that Levine was working on

---

[14] OPR completed its report of the results of its investigation of Burke's involvement in the disclosure of the Avila memorandum on July 27, 2012. OPR concluded that Burke directed or authorized the Avila memorandum to be sent to The New York Times in violation of Department media relations rules, and committed misconduct. OPR also found that as a lawyer whose client was the Department, Burke violated Rules of Professional Conduct in Arizona and the District of Columbia when he failed to provide accurate information to and otherwise misled the Deputy Attorney General, and when he directed or authorized the disclosure of confidential information (the Avila memorandum) without his client's consent. On October 25, 2012, the Chief of the Department's Professional Misconduct Review Unit upheld all of OPR's misconduct findings after considering Burke's appeal. OPR subsequently referred its findings to the Arizona and District of Columbia Bars.

[15] As noted earlier, Burke was interviewed by congressional investigators on December 13, 2011, about several matters pertaining to Operation Fast and Furious, including his disclosure of the Dodson memorandum to a reporter. At the OIG's request, the staff of the House Committee on Oversight and Government Reform provided a copy of Burke's transcribed interview and we cite to testimony Burke provided to congressional investigators in this report.

several stories, including one that involved a memorandum Dodson had written that, from Levine's perspective, contradicted Dodson's congressional testimony about the tactic of "walking" firearms to build an investigation. Burke said that Levine asked Burke whether he had seen the memorandum, to which Burke replied he had. Levine then asked for a copy of it, and Burke provided it by e-mailing the Dodson memorandum from his personal account to a friend of Burke's in Washington, D.C., who in turn provided a hard copy of the document directly to Levine.[16]

Congressional investigators asked Burke why he did not send the Dodson memorandum directly to Levine. Burke acknowledged that would have been the easier method, but said that he had some concern about the document being easily circulated if it was on the Fox e-mail system. However, Burke also stated that he did not have any arrangement with Levine about not forwarding the memorandum.

According to e-mails reviewed by the OIG, on June 28, 2011, Burke forwarded to his private e-mail account Cunningham's April 5, 2011, e-mail that included as an attachment the Dodson memorandum. Burke took this action one day after he had been admonished by Deputy Attorney General Cole for lying to him about the leak of the Avila memorandum, had been put on notice by Cole that such disclosures should not occur, and had told Cole that he took responsibility for his office's disclosure of the Avila memorandum. Burke also was aware by this date that his conduct in connection with the disclosure of the Avila memorandum was under investigation by OPR.

Burke was asked by congressional investigators why he gave the Dodson memorandum to Levine. Burke replied,

> Because he, A, he seemed to know what already was in it; B, I was assuming it was going to be released at some point anyway. I was under the impression that it had gone to the Hill and that I was giving basically a time advantage.

Burke stated that he had been told by Cunningham that the memorandum had been provided to Congress, which Burke said he later learned was incorrect.[17] As noted earlier, congressional investigators

---

[16] The friend Burke identified, who is not a Department employee, declined our request for a voluntary interview. The OIG does not have authority to compel an interview for an individual who is not a Department employee.

[17] On January 19, 2012, in response to a deposition scheduled by congressional investigators, Cunningham asserted his Fifth Amendment privilege not to be compelled to be a witness against himself. Cunningham subsequently resigned from the U.S.

were given access to the Dodson memorandum on June 21, 2011, but were not provided a copy of the document. Burke denied to congressional investigators that he provided the memorandum to Levine "to undermine Agent Dodson's veracity or testimony." Burke also acknowledged that he should not have disclosed the document to Levine – that "[i]t was a mistake" – but said he did not think of it as a mistake at the time he did it.

On June 29, the day after Burke forwarded the Dodson memorandum to his private e-mail account, Levine sent an e-mail to a colleague at Fox News, William LaJeunesse, stating,

> I know you've had contact before with John Dobson [sic], and I'm working on a story that I hope he can offer some insight/response to. Essentially, I got a copy of a proposal he made in May 2010 to go undercover and investigate gun traffickers. Here are some key quotes/bits from his proposal
> . . .

Levine's e-mail provided verbatim excerpts from Dodson's memorandum and contrasted these with excerpts from Dodson's congressional testimony. The verbatim excerpts included "[redacted]" notations indicating where material had been redacted from the source document. These notations tracked the redactions the Department made in the version of the memorandum made available to congressional investigators on June 21 and that the Department indicated in the version provided to the U.S. Attorney's Office on June 22.[18] Levine's e-mail concluded,

> I'm hoping [Dodson] has some info/context he can offer about this. On its face, the two things (proposal vs. recent

---

Attorney's Office and declined our request for a follow-up interview on matters related to Operation Fast and Furious.

[18] The version of the Dodson memorandum that Burke sent to his personal e-mail address on June 28 was the unredacted version Cunningham had sent to Burke and several others on April 5, 2011. As noted above, a version indicating the Department's redactions to the document was provided to the U.S. Attorney's Office on June 22. Burke told Congressional investigators that the memorandum and other documents had been sent to the U.S. Attorney's Office for review as part of the production process, and that Cunningham told him the memorandum had been produced to Congress. Congressional investigators did not ask Burke what version he provided to Levine or how the redactions to the document were identified, and Burke declined our request for an interview so we could not ask. The friend in Washington, D.C., to whom Burke said he e-mailed the memorandum and who in turn personally provided a hard copy of the document to Levine also declined our request for an interview.

testimony) seem to be different, but I'm hoping/assuming he has an explanation or can offer info I don't have about it.

LaJenuesse forwarded Levine's e-mail to Dodson that same day, June 29.

Dodson told the OIG that he spoke to Levine by telephone about the memorandum after receiving the e-mail from LaJenuesse. According to Dodson, Levine told him he had obtained the memorandum from "a source at Justice." Dodson said he told Levine that the undercover investigation was in fact a proposal by his supervisor and that all Dodson did was author the document and provide it to his supervisor. Dodson told us that Levine seemed to accept this explanation and that he told Dodson he did not think he was going to further pursue a story about the memorandum. Dodson also told us that Levine said the memorandum was probably provided to him with the intent of contradicting Dodson's congressional testimony.

On the same date that Levine's e-mail was forwarded to Dodson – June 29, 2011 – Levine also exchanged e-mails with Tracy Schmaler, the Director of the Department's Office of Public Affairs. Levine inquired, "If I were to get a copy of a proposal from John Dodson to 'walk' guns to criminals, would you care to comment?" Schmaler replied, "Let's cross that bridge when you come to it. I want to see the alleged evidence." Levine responded, "Time to cross that bridge." Schmaler forwarded the e-mail exchange to the Office of the Deputy Attorney General and told us that she did not provide Levine with a comment about the information he said he had regarding Dodson.

D.   Burke admits to disclosure of Dodson memorandum

As described earlier, the OIG initiated its investigation of the disclosure of the Dodson memorandum in July 2011 in response to a complaint from Dodson's attorney. On August 12, 2011, the day after the OIG issued requests for information to various Department components, including the U.S. Attorney's Office, Burke contacted Associate Deputy Attorney General Steven Reich and told him that he had provided the information at issue to a reporter.[19] Reich said Burke also told him that he did not know at the time he provided the information to the reporter that the Dodson memorandum had been made available only for review by congressional investigators. According to Reich, Burke also said that the reporter already seemed to have the

---

[19] Reich was responsible for helping to coordinate the Department's response to congressional oversight and related investigations by other entities.

Dodson memorandum or had seen a copy of it, and that Burke therefore did not think he was doing anything inappropriate by sharing information with a reporter who already had it or had seen it. However, Burke also told Reich that he thought he (Burke) should resign as U.S. Attorney.

Reich said he told Burke that he would report their conversation to Deputy Attorney General Cole and that someone would get back in touch with him. Reich said he promptly briefed Cole about the conversation with Burke.

Cole told the OIG that after Reich briefed him, he spoke with Burke by telephone on August 12 and again on August 13. Cole said both conversations focused more on Burke's decision to resign than on specifics about Burke's disclosure of the memorandum. According to the notes Cole took of the first call, Burke stated that he was ready to step down as U.S. Attorney and that he had given the Dodson memorandum to the reporter. The notes also indicate that Burke told Cole his resignation would be in the best interest of his office and would also help the Department. The first call ended with Burke telling Cole he wanted to think about the matter overnight and the two agreed to speak again the following day. Cole said the two in fact did speak on August 13 and that during the call Burke affirmed his decision to resign. Cole stated that he and Burke then discussed the timing of the announcement of the resignation.[20]

Cole told the OIG that he was disappointed in Burke for leaking the Dodson memorandum and that his disappointment was compounded by Burke's role in the earlier leak of the Avila memorandum to The New York Times. Cole's notes of the August 12 call with Burke state, "another horrible incident of bad judgment six to seven weeks ago."

Burke ended the August 13 call with Cole by telling him that he would report the leak of the Dodson memorandum to the OIG. As noted earlier, Burke in fact did this on August 16, during a short telephone conversation with an OIG investigative counsel. Burke told the investigative counsel that he was the person the OIG was looking for and that he was self-reporting. He told the OIG that he had a conversation with a reporter who was asking questions about a memorandum describing an undercover operation conducted by Dodson. According to Burke, the reporter knew all the details pertaining to the operation and asked Burke if he knew about the memorandum. Burke said he located

---

[20] Burke announced his resignation as U.S. Attorney on August 30, 2011. The resignation took effect that day.

the memorandum and produced it to the reporter. Burke told the investigative counsel that he was "unabashed" about providing the document and did not believe he did anything illegal.

Burke gave similar accounts of his conduct to the First Assistant and the Executive Assistant in the U.S. Attorney's Office for the District of Arizona after the OIG initiated its investigation. Both told the OIG that Burke told them he had provided the Dodson memorandum to a reporter after being asked for it. Burke also told them that the reporter was already familiar with the information in the document and that Burke did not think it was improper to provide it to the reporter because he believed at that time the document had already been produced to congressional investigators and was therefore public, an understanding Burke came to learn was incorrect.

The First Assistant and Executive Assistant told us that Burke had been frustrated by some of Dodson's June 2011 congressional testimony about Operation Fast and Furious. The First Assistant stated,

> I think [Burke] thought [Dodson] was not necessarily completely sincere when he was so critical about the tactics that were used, alleged tactics in Fast and Furious when he was someone who is really trying to push those same tactics in his own case.

Similarly, the Executive Assistant told us that she understood Burke disclosed the document to help the U.S. Attorney's Office defend against what Burke considered hypocritical criticisms being made by Dodson.

Burke also admitted his conduct to the OIG through his counsel. In a letter to the Acting Inspector General dated November 8, 2011, Burke's counsel stated that Burke's intention in disclosing the memorandum in response to the reporter's request "was to give context to the information that the reporter already had in order to explain that investigations similar to Operation Fast and Furious had been previously proposed by ATF." Burke's counsel also asserted that the memorandum "was not subject to any limitations on disclosure under the Freedom of Information Act" because the underlying investigation was closed, the memorandum did not contain any Grand Jury or otherwise classified information, and Congress had already released to the public other reports from the investigation.

Our investigation did not identify any other Department of Justice employee who disclosed the Dodson memorandum to the media. Each of the 150 Department employees from whom we requested declarations stated that they did not discuss information in the Dodson memorandum with any member of the media, and did not provide the Dodson memorandum or information from the Dodson memorandum to any member of the media. Five declarants stated in their declarations that they had some direct knowledge of the disclosure of the Dodson memorandum. As described above, four of those five – Deputy Attorney General Cole, Associate Deputy Attorney General Reich, and the First Assistant and Executive Assistant from the U.S. Attorney's Office – reported that their direct knowledge consisted of Burke's admissions to them that he had disclosed the memorandum to a reporter. The fifth declarant – Tracey Schmaler, the Director of the Department's Office of Public Affairs – told us about the e-mail inquiry she received on June 29, 2011, from Levine about information he claimed to have regarding an investigation where Dodson attempted to "walk guns."

IV.   OIG ANALYSIS

As described above, Burke admitted that he provided a copy of the Dodson memorandum to Fox News reporter Levine. We did not identify any other Department employee who disclosed the memorandum to Levine or to any other member of the media.

We concluded that Burke's disclosure of the Dodson memorandum to Levine violated Department rules pertaining to media relations contained in the United States Attorneys' Manual, Sections1-7.210, 1-7.320, and 1-7.330. As described in Section II.B. of this report, these provisions require that OPA be kept informed of requests of national media organizations that relate to matters of national importance or significance, and that any media efforts of a Department component that relate to such matters be coordinated with OPA.

These Department rules clearly applied here. Burke disclosed the memorandum to a reporter who worked for Fox News, a national media organization. Further, Burke clearly knew at the time he disclosed the memorandum to Levine in June 2011 that Operation Fast and Furious was a matter of national importance. The Fast and Furious case had been the subject of separate congressional and OIG inquiries for months and had gained significant attention from the media and the public. Burke also knew there were extensive and at times contentious discussions between the Department and Congress about the production of documents and that final decisions about what materials would be disclosed were being made by senior leadership offices in Washington, D.C. Under these circumstances, Burke was required by the U.S. Attorney's Manual to inform OPA of Levine's request for information and to coordinate any media efforts he or his office might make with respect to Levine's request. We found no evidence that Burke did this. In fact,

Burke told congressional investigators that he did not discuss his decision to disclose the memorandum to Levine with anybody from OPA.

As noted earlier, Burke declined our request to interview him about the disclosure of the Dodson memorandum and therefore we did not receive from him a detailed explanation for his conduct. However, Burke told congressional investigators and others that at the time he provided the document to Levine, he believed Levine had already obtained or seen the document and the document had already been produced to Congress. Burke also told congressional investigators that it was a mistake to provide the document to Levine, but that he did not think it was at the time he did it.

We rejected this explanation. First, regardless of whether Burke in fact believed Levine or Congress already had the memorandum, that belief would not excuse his failure to comply with Department policy concerning media inquiries.[21] The USAM policy is unambiguous that communications with national media organizations regarding matters of national significance must be coordinated with OPA. Thus, Burke should have informed OPA of the request whether or not he believed Levine or Congress already had the memorandum.

Second, we found that Burke disclosed the Dodson memorandum despite knowing he was under investigation at the very same time by OPR for virtually the same alleged misconduct – the unauthorized disclosure of the Avila memorandum to the media. Indeed, his disclosure of the Dodson memorandum occurred on the day after the Deputy Attorney General of the United States chastised Burke for lying to the Deputy Attorney General about his involvement in the disclosure of the Avila memorandum and put him on notice that such disclosures should not happen. We do not believe that under these circumstances, Burke thought he could release the Dodson memorandum to a reporter without prior consultation with and approval from OPA and the Office of the Deputy Attorney General.

Third, the manner in which Burke provided the Dodson memorandum to Levine demonstrated to us that Burke was aware his actions were improper, particularly in light of Burke's recent experience in improperly disclosing the Avila memorandum to The New York Times. As described earlier, that disclosure was quickly traced back to the U.S.

---

[21] We do not resolve the issue of whether Burke's asserted belief is relevant to any separate investigation of whether he disclosed confidential client information in violation of the Rules of Professional Conduct in the states in which he is licensed to practice law. We are providing this memorandum to OPR for a determination of whether Burke's conduct should be referred to Bar Counsel.

Attorney's Office because the banner on the image of the document indicated the date and time the document had been facsimiled from the office. In contrast, Burke told congressional investigators he e-mailed the Dodson memorandum from his personal e-mail account to a friend in Washington, D.C., so that his friend would hand-deliver a hard copy of the document to the reporter. We believe that by providing the memorandum indirectly to the reporter through a friend and from his personal e-mail account, Burke took calculated measures to reduce the possibility that the disclosure could be traced back to him and to the U.S. Attorney's Office. Burke acknowledged that it would have been easier to send the Dodson memorandum directly to Levine, but said he transmitted the Dodson memorandum through a friend because he had some concern about the document being circulated on the Fox e-mail system. Given that Burke intended delivery of the memorandum to a national news reporter, and the ease with which a document can be converted to a portable document format (pdf) for attachment to an e-mail, we did not find Burke's explanation credible.

We also concluded that Burke's disclosure of the Dodson memorandum to Levine was likely motivated by a desire to undermine Dodson's public criticisms of Operation Fast and Furious. Although Burke denied to congressional investigators that he had any retaliatory motive for his actions, we found substantial evidence to the contrary.[22]

First, we found the timing of the disclosure coupled with Burke's apparent frustration regarding Dodson's testimony to Congress to be strong indicators of his state of mind and motivation. Both the First Assistant and the Executive Assistant in the U.S. Attorney's Office told us that Burke was frustrated with Dodson's June 15, 2011, public congressional testimony that was highly critical of the handling of Operation Fast and Furious. The First Assistant told us that Burke felt Dodson was "not necessarily completely sincere" when he criticized the tactics used in Operation Fast and Furious while proposing to use those very tactics in his own investigation. The Executive Assistant told us that she understood Burke disclosed the document to help the U.S. Attorney's Office defend against what were considered hypocritical criticisms being made by Dodson. That disclosure occurred less than two weeks after Dodson's public testimony before Congress.

Burke expressed similar feelings just two months earlier regarding what he considered to be Dodson's hypocrisy. As we described earlier, CBS News published a story on March 3, 2011, that featured an

---

[22] We did not analyze the case as a whistleblower retaliation claim because the OIG does not have jurisdiction over ATF whistleblower retaliation claims.

interview with Dodson in which he stated that ATF was intentionally allowing firearms to go to Mexico, a tactic referred to as "walking" guns, and that he was ordered not to take any action to stop the firearms and that the tactic was approved by Department officials. The story also reported that Sen. Grassley began investigating Operation Fast and Furious after his office spoke to Dodson and several other ATF sources. About one month later, in response to Criminal Chief Cunningham's April 5, 2011, e-mail identifying to the Department the Dodson memorandum as potentially responsive to the recently issued congressional subpoena, Burke stated,

> Yep. Unbelievable. This guy called Grassley and CBS to unearth what he in fact was proposing to do by himself. When you thought the hypocrisy of this whole matter had hit the limit already.

Second, according to Burke's account of his conversation with Levine, Burke believed that Levine was working on a story that would expose what Burke considered Dodson's hypocrisy. Burke said that Levine told him the story involved a memorandum Dodson had written that, from Levine's perspective, contradicted Dodson's congressional testimony about the tactic of "walking" firearms to build an investigation. Indeed, Burke's counsel stated in a letter sent to the OIG on November 8, 2011, that "[Burke's] intention [in providing the Dodson memorandum to a reporter] was to give context to information that the reporter already had to explain that investigations similar to Operation Fast and Furious had been previously proposed by ATF." In other words, Burke's intention in disclosing the memorandum was to show that ATF, through Dodson, proposed in another investigation the very tactics that Dodson and other agents were criticizing ATF for using in Operation Fast and Furious. We believe that this explanation, taken together with the other evidence cited above, demonstrate that Burke's conduct in disclosing the memorandum to Levine was likely motivated by his desire to undermine Dodson's public criticisms.

Third, in connection with the Department's review of the disclosure of the Avila memorandum, Burke provided information to the Department regarding his role in providing the memorandum to The New York Times and whether he misled Deputy Attorney General Cole during their telephone conversation on June 16, 2011. Burke stated that the "unprecedented scrutiny and investigations while weathering scurrilous media attacks" concerning Operation Fast and Furious had been a "nightmare" and resulted in a lack of confidence by Burke that the Department was protecting the interests of his office. Burke was critical of OPA, as well as the Office of the Deputy Attorney General and Office of Legislative Affairs, and stated that "several U.S. Attorney's [] commented

to me that the Department was throwing my office under the bus . . ."
Burke's statements to the Department reflected a belief that he could not
rely on the Department to respond to criticism of his office's handling of
the Fast and Furious investigation, and we found that he responded to
this belief by deciding to defend the office himself through, in part, the
unauthorized disclosure of information to the media. The story that
Burke believed Levine was working on provided Burke with a vehicle to
do just that.

In sum, we found that Burke violated Department policy when he
provided the Dodson memorandum to Fox News reporter Levine without
Department approval, and that his explanations for why he did not
believe his actions were improper were not credible. We believe this
misconduct to be particularly egregious because of Burke's apparent
effort to undermine the credibility of Dodson's significant public
disclosures about the failures in Operation Fast and Furious. We further
believe that the seriousness of Burke's actions are aggravated by the fact
that they were taken within days after he told Deputy Attorney General
Cole that he took responsibility for his office's earlier unauthorized
disclosure of a document to The New York Times, and after Cole put him
on notice that such disclosures should not occur. Burke also knew at
the time of his disclosure of the Dodson memorandum that he was under
investigation by OPR for his conduct in connection with the earlier
disclosure to The New York Times. As a high-level Department official,
Burke knew his obligations to abide by Department policies and his duty
to follow the instructions of the Deputy Attorney General, who was
Burke's immediate supervisor.

We found Burke's conduct in disclosing the Dodson memorandum
to be inappropriate for a Department employee and wholly unbefitting a
U.S. Attorney. We are referring to OPR our finding that Burke violated
Department policy in disclosing the Dodson memorandum to a member
of the media for a determination of whether Burke's conduct violated the
Rules of Professional Conduct for the state bars in which Burke is a
member.

www.ingramcontent.com/pod-product-compliance
Lightning Source LLC
Chambersburg PA
CBHW081825170526
45167CB00008B/3553